To Colin. Never stop exploring this weird, weird world. — R.M.

For M.K., my best friend. — J.S.

Text copyright © 2022 by Rosemary Mosco
Illustrations copyright © 2022 by Jacob Souva

Tundra Books, an imprint of Penguin Random House Canada Young Readers,
a division of Penguin Random House of Canada Limited

Library and Archives Canada Cataloguing in Publication

Title: Flowers are pretty... weird! / Rosemary Mosco ; [illustrated by] Jacob Souva.
Names: Mosco, Rosemary, author. | Souva, Jacob, illustrator.
Identifiers: Canadiana (print) 20200352954 | Canadiana (ebook) 20200353047 |
ISBN 9780735265943 (hardcover) | ISBN 9780735265950 (EPUB)
Subjects: LCSH: Flowers—Juvenile literature. |
LCSH: Flowers—Pictorial works—Juvenile literature.
Classification: LCC QK49 .M67 2022 | DDC j582.13—dc23

Published simultaneously in the United States of America by Tundra Books of Northern
New York, an imprint of Penguin Random House Canada Young Readers, a division of
Penguin Random House of Canada Limited

Library of Congress Control Number: 2020947311

Acknowledgments: Special thanks to Dr. Chris Thorogood. — R.M.

Edited by Peter Phillips and Elizabeth Kribs
Designed by John Martz and Leah Springate
The artwork in this book was created digitally.
The text was set in Colby.

Printed in China

www.penguinrandomhouse.ca

1 2 3 4 5   26 25 24 23 22

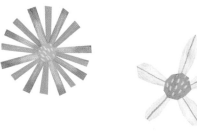

tundra | Penguin
Random House
TUNDRA BOOKS

Flowers ARE PRETTY WEIRD!

ROSEMARY MOSCO

ILLUSTRATED BY
JACOB SOUVA

tundra

Hi! I'm a bee.

And there's **one thing**
that a bee adores more
than anything else . . .

FLOWERS!

I love them. Bee-lieve me, I do.

I love their bright colors and soft petals.

I *especially* love their sweet nectar.

Yum.

FLOWERS ILLUSTRATED

Maybe you don't think flowers are exciting.

Maybe they even seem boring to you
but not to me.

If you hang out with flowers as much as I do,
you start to learn some strange things.

You see, flowers aren't just pretty . . .

They're pretty **weird**.

They're weird enough to make your four wings quiver.

(If you're a bee, that is.)

Flowers are full of opposites.

Some flowers are huge, but some are tiny.
Some are tasty, but some are poisonous.
Some smell nice, but some are as stinky as old socks.

See? They're not boring at all!

Bee honest — do you think I'm lying?

Well, I can **prove** it.

I can show you some really weird flowers.

If you want to join me, **turn the page**.

If you don't, **close this book** and buzz right off.

Which will it bee?

Oh, thank you for bee-lieving in me!
I won't let you down.

Some flowers are cute.

They look like ducks
or doves
or monkeys.

DOVE ORCHID

LARGE DUCK ORCHID

MONKEY ORCHID

GHOST FLOWER

PELICAN FLOWER

WHITE BAT FLOWER

But some flowers
are spooky.

They look like ghosts
or bats
or a monster's mouth.

Some flowers are yummy.

You can sprinkle them on a salad
for a tasty treat.

Other flowers are poisonous.

Their poison stops bugs from eating them.

They'll make you sick too. Don't eat any flower without asking a grown-up first.

Those are just a **few** of the many weird flowers.

Truth bee told, I've seen weirder.

I've seen flowers so weird, they'll make
your six legs shiver.

(If you're a bee, that is.)

If you want me to show you some even stranger flowers, **turn the page**.

If you don't, **shut this book**, and I'll mind my own beeswax.

You stuck around! You're sweet as honey.

Here's a secret: plants need to spread **pollen** from flower
to flower. That's how they make more plants.
Insects like me help carry this pollen.

me

some
BEETLE

Some flowers open their petals wide.

Oxeye Daisies show their faces
to the sky. Beetles and flies and
other insects spread their pollen.

But some flowers never open their petals.

Closed Bottle Gentians stay shut up tight forever.

Only big bees can squeeze inside. Big bees are best at spreading this flower's pollen.

POLLeN ROCKS!

POLLeN in theRe

(BeE Butt LOL)

noT me

So Pretty

no Relation

Most flowers bloom in the daytime.

California Poppies open their petals in the morning light.

They shimmer in the sun.
Bees and butterflies spread their pollen.

FUZZY moth →

SoOOo COOOL !

But some flowers only bloom
in the nighttime.

Dragon Fruit flowers wait until it's dark and cool.

They open in the shadows. Moths spread their pollen.

COOL!

Some flowers live in the sky.

Twisted-leaved Air Plants grow
on tall, tall trees.

Hummingbirds spread their pollen.

SUPER FAST

And some flowers live under the ground.

Western Underground Orchids hide in the soil.

Termites spread their pollen.

Monique

Roger

Mike

Tobias

BURIED TREASURE!

Those are some pretty strange flowers.

But I've seen stranger ones.

I've seen flowers so strange they'll make
your two antennae tremble.

(If you're a bee, that is.)

If you want me to show you the wildest flowers of all, **turn the page**.

If you don't, **drop this book** and go play with some pollen.

You bee-lieved me again!
I'm the luckiest bee you'll ever see.

Most flowers smell good.

Roses have a sweet scent.

They use their perfume to attract
butterflies and bees.

But some flowers stink.

Starfish flowers smell like dead meat, and some *Orchidantha* flowers stink like horse poop.

They use their stench to attract flies and beetles that eat yucky things.

Some flowers are tiny.

See this dot? A Duckweed flower is this small. It's smaller than a grain of salt.

·

B-TUBE

But some flowers are gigantic.

The Corpse Lily is wider than the tire on a truck.

(And guess what? It stinks too.
Like rotten meat. Eww.)

Well, I hope you bee-lieve me now!

Flowers aren't just pretty.

They're so much more.

And that's why I love them.

You're pretty and weird
and so much more too.

And *psst*,
that's why I love you.

About Some of the Strangest Flowers in This Book

WHITE BAT FLOWER

Scientists Call It: *Tacca integrifolia*

This bizarre flower is a cousin of the yam. Some people think that it looks like a bat. Other people see a cat with long whiskers. Take a close look. Which do you see: a bat or a cat?

WHERE TO SEE IT: SOUTHEAST ASIA

WOLFSBANE

Scientists Call It: *Aconitum napellus*

This flower is beautiful but poisonous. It is also called Monkshood because it looks like a purple-blue hood that a teeny tiny person might wear on their head. It's pretty stylish!

WHERE TO SEE IT: WESTERN AND CENTRAL EUROPE

CLOSED BOTTLE GENTIAN

Scientists Call It: *Gentiana andrewsii*

When autumn comes, the Bottle Gentian blooms. The flower never opens, but bumblebees are big and strong enough to push their way between its petals to drink the sweet nectar inside.

WHERE TO SEE IT: EASTERN NORTH AMERICA

WESTERN UNDERGROUND ORCHID

Scientists Call It: *Rhizanthella gardneri*

This amazing plant has no roots or leaves. It lives underground, which makes it hard to find! We don't know how many Western Underground Orchids are hiding under the soil right now.

WHERE TO SEE IT: WESTERN AUSTRALIA

DRAGON FRUIT

Scientists Call It: *Hylocereus undatus*

Not only does this cool plant bloom at night, but it also makes spiky red fruits that look like dragon eggs. Cut open the fruits, and you'll see bright white flesh with tiny black seeds.

WHERE TO SEE IT: CENTRAL AMERICA AND ASIA

DUCKWEED

Scientists Call It: *Wolffia globosa*

A Duckweed plant is teeny tiny — it weighs about as much as two of your eyelashes. It doesn't have any roots, so it's not stuck in one place. Instead, it floats around on the surface of a swamp or pond.

WHERE TO SEE IT: ASIA, NORTH AMERICA AND SOUTH AMERICA

CORPSE LILY

Scientists Call It: *Rafflesia arnoldii*

This plant is sneaky. It lives inside a vine and steals the vine's food. You'll only see it when it makes its gigantic flower, which stinks like rotten meat.

WHERE TO SEE IT: SOUTHEAST ASIA